Where

Glory

Dwells

Where

Sanctuaries I Remember

Glory

Stephen Redmond SJ

Dwells

VERITAS

Published 2003 by
Veritas Publications
7/8 Lower Abbey Street
Dublin 1
Email publications@veritas.ie
Website www.veritas.ie

ISBN 1 85390 673 5

A catalogue record for this book is available from the British Library.

Cover design by Syd Bluett
Printed in the Republic of Ireland by Betaprint Ltd, Dublin

Veritas books are printed on paper made from the wood pulp of managed forests. For every tree felled, at least one tree is planted, thereby renewing natural resources.

I have loved, O Lord, the beauty of thy house
and the place where thy glory dwelleth

Psalm 25/26:8

In tribute to all the people in church mentioned in this book

CONTENTS

FOREWORD

All religious communities have their sanctuaries, their holy places. What is specific to Christian sanctuaries is that they derive from and centre on the unique revelation of the divine glory and presence that we call the Christ-event. In these sanctuaries believers thankfully acknowledge the glory and the presence, celebrate the Event and take part in its ongoing drama of grace.

This book gives some account of the role of such places in my life. In them I have prayed, officiated, received the sacraments, listened to the scriptures, met and noticed people, learned something of history and art and of the tradition I come from, shared in music and relished the occasional comic interlude. I hope I have appreciated them as, above all else, places for the meeting of the Eucharistic Lord and his people in sacrifice, communion and presence.

Much enjoyment and affection (and, I venture to say, gratitude) went into the writing of *Where Glory Dwells*, and much wrestling with rhymes into the poems that highlight some significant memories.

I hope that the book will evoke similar memories for its readers and enhance their appreciation of holy places in their

own lives. May it help them towards the Sanctuary where they
will experience in eternal joy the Glory that they now believe in
and hope for.

Stephen Redmond SJ
John Austin House
Dublin
January 2003

MUSICAL FOREWORD

The Temple of the Lord

Ezechiel 47:1-12

I saw light come pouring as I passed the temple by
and it gave new loveliness to land and sea and sky
and I knew the Lord was living, never more to die
O sing glory, glory alleluia!

I heard song and music as I passed the temple door
soft as wind in summer, strong as storm upon the shore
and I knew that love was living there forevermore
O sing glory, glory alleluia!

Come and enter, come and fill the temple of the Lord
for your Fountain's here, your Light, your Nourishment and Word
He's the Song to fill your heart with freedom's lovely chord
O sing glory, glory alleluia!

Deeply I Adore You

Adoro Te Devote

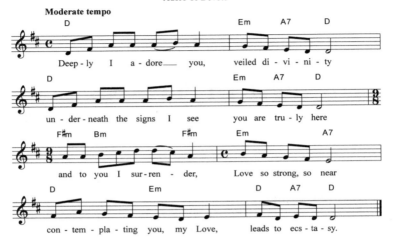

Thomas saw your hands and side: wounds I do not see
yet like him I call you Lord, call you God, adore
Jesus, let me believe in you ever more and more
Jesus, let me hope in you, love you utterly

Sacrament of Calvary, Lover through and through
Sacrament of Easter Day, gift of Living Bread
let me savour your sweetness, purified and fed
giving thanks for evermore, drawing life from you

Now I turn to you in faith: you are veiled from me
hidden Jesus, hear my prayer, give this longed-for grace
bring me out of the shadowlands, let me see your face
in your glory let me find joy eternally

1
EARLY YEARS

Family: Ballsbridge

The Redmonds of Ballsbridge Bakery, Dublin had two special church-related domestic items: a screen and a car. The screen had been the door of either a tabernacle or a receptacle for church requisites: I still remember the day I became aware of the keyhole and the beautifully carved IHS and grapes motif. The car had belonged to a priest and had doubtless on occasion carried the Blessed Sacrament: a kind of mobile church. We were strongly church-related ourselves, having three local parish churches to choose from for our Sunday devotions.

The first church I visited was none of these, but Saint Andrew's Westland Row where I was baptised on 29 December 1919, not far from the painting of Saint Thomas Becket's martyrdom donated to the church by the great Daniel O'Connell. December 29 is Thomas's feastday and the anniversary of his death. Because of all this coincidence he is understandably one of my patron saints. Many years later I was to visit the scene of his martyrdom in the great church of Canterbury.

Saint Mary's, Haddington Road is special to me: there my parents were married and there I made my first confession and communion from the Holy Faith school down the road. I remember pretty precisely where I knelt for communion and quite clearly the word that went round that one of us had received twice. I recall the lyrical text on the Bishop Donnelly memorial: 'I have loved, O Lord, the beauty of thy house and the place where thy glory dwelleth'. It seems to have said more to me than I realised at the time.

Everything seemed to be on the grand scale: the carved altar rails, the high pulpit, the crucifix-centred Great War memorial with its poignant list of names, the three-dimensional stations of the Cross, the saints in stained-glass, the mighty organ. Even the gentle Saint Anthony was a towering figure. But the impact of all this did not prevent me from having free reads of CTS pamphlets, especially the work of J. Bernard McCarthy. And I still hear the distant echo of the *Pange Lingua* of the Corpus Christi procession in the church grounds.

Three Haddington Road persons come to mind: the unflappable sacristan, an ecclesiastical Jeeves, marshalling clergy and altar boys with equal aplomb; Father John Hooke who encouraged me about becoming a priest, telling me to get a mysterious thing called 'matriculation' or 'matric'; and Bishop Francis Wall who became my confessor: a man of limitless kindness and patience, a true friend in the faith.

I move on to Donnybrook Church. This Edward Pugin-Ashlin church dates to the 1860s and was dedicated to the Sacred Heart in reparation for the misdoings associated with the recently suppressed Donnybrook Fair. Inset into a transept wall is a cross from the penal-day chapel which stood near the present Garda station. It had a homelier atmosphere than Haddington Road: the stations of the Cross had pictures, not reliefs, the organ had a softer sound and the sacristan (whose moustache, to a conservative juvenile eye, did not go with a cassock and surplice) did not inspire awe.

The first Donnybrook parish priest I recall was the austere and rather terrifying Canon Dunne. His successor was the more affable Monsignor-Canon Moloney who administered the sacrament of penance with remarkable rapidity and presided at a crowded monthly 'Golden Hour' in honour of the Sacred Heart.

My most dramatic memory of that church is of a Sunday when I made a declaration of independence and went alone (and fasting from midnight according to the rule of the time) to receive communion at an early Mass (communion was not given at later Masses). In the church I got faint, began to panic, looked around in desperation and there was my mother right behind me. She had followed me all the way to the church.

A person I associate with Donnybrook Church is a dear friend of my youth: Edward (Teddy) Byrne of Home Villas near Herbert Park who was or had been a Mass-server there. It may well have been at the altar that he came to think of becoming a priest. There was an unaffected and almost radiant goodness about him. We were both ardent fans of Deanna Durbin, the singing movie star. He died in 1941 while a student at All Hallows College, Dublin. I visit his grave there occasionally and think of him when I pass through Donnybrook or go out to the university campus at Belfield where we played tennis with him usually winning.

On to Sandymount. The beautifully named Star of the Sea Church (mentioned by Joyce in *Ulysses*) had a sacristan who wizardlike could light a whole line of candles with one sweep of a taper. It also had an operatically-inclined choir and an organist with a strong weakness for the tremolo. My sister Norah who liked opera used to bring me to Mass there.

I recall the lit-up shrine of the Christ of Limpias with the agonised Face against the renaissance red. There was the window of the risen Lord appearing in a radiant silvery robe to

Thomas. I thought of this robe as his 'Sunday suit' and of his duller clothes in an adjoining pre-Resurrecton scene as his 'weekday suit'. I see now that this was quite an insight into the meaning of the Resurrection. It was on Sandymount strand one Sunday after Mass that I told my mother that I was thinking of becoming a priest.

Like so many mothers of her generation she was a great Mass-goer and church visitor and was very much in the Irish tradition of frequent vocal prayer: only God knows how much her prayers engraced the rest of us. One of her haunts was the chapel of the Poor Clares in Simmonscourt Road near the Royal Dublin Society showgrounds. In time it became a haunt of mine too. It had two tabernacles: the 'standard' one and above it a larger one in which the monstranced Host was kept, facing the nuns' choir. The 'golden' door of this second tabernacle was the focal point of the chapel: it was a masterpiece of church décor, contributing much to the atmosphere of adoration and faith. I recall making some sort of offering about the priesthood at the Lourdes grotto in the grounds.

My father's favourite church was the Carmelite Saint Teresa's in Clarendon Street. A historic church this, dating to the 1790s. In its early years it was the scene of meetings concerned with 'the Catholic question' with Daniel O'Connell as their leading light. Its artistic centrepiece is Hogan's master sculpture of the Christus in death. My father went to confession in this church. He had, I seem to recall, a devotion to Saint Thérèse of Lisieux (they were contemporaries, both born in the 1870s): it may have started at her Clarendon shrine.

He and I were together at the final Mass of the Eucharistic Congress in Dublin in 1932. It was a feast of sight and sound: the Fifteen Acres in the Phoenix Park turned into a vast church with a congregation of a million; the white expanse of the domed altar and flanking colonnades; the voice of Pope Pius XI from Rome; John McCormack singing 'Panis Angelicus'; at the consecration the clunk of Saint Patrick's Bell, spanning fifteen centuries of the Eucharist in Ireland; the soldiers' sunlit swords held high in homage from consecration to communion with incredible discipline and style.

There was the annual Holy Thursday pilgrimage to the seven altars of repose, the prayer being accompanied by critical appraisal and comparison of devotional décor: those were the days when sacristans delighted in candles, flowers, filigree and lace. A special eucharistic locale was the Marie Reparatrice Convent in Merrion Square where Georgian grandeur had been adapted to devotion with the Host enthroned in the light of countless candles. Years later a new chapel was built around the corner in Fitzwilliam Street and I found myself giving retreat talks in the room where I had once prayed. In an inspired (?) moment I mentioned my previous association with the place and may have suggested that it had something to do with my being a priest. The sisters perked up, purred prayerfully and those of Reparatrice looked at me with a certain proprietorial interest.

A church of my early years with a strong family connection was Saint Mochta's at Porterstown, County Dublin: a small late nineteenth century Romanesque granite-fronted church on high ground overlooking the Liffey from the north. My father's first marriage took place there. The bridesmaid was Teresa Lennon who was to be his second wife and my mother. She came from this area and would have attended Mass in Saint Mochta's in her young days.

My father dreamt of building a house near the church for his retirement to be called 'Mellifont', a name he delighted in. He never achieved his dream, but when he bought a house for his newly-married daughter Norah and her husband to live in, 'Mellifont' was its name and, I am glad to say, still is.

Family: Sallins

I have early years memories of the chapel of ease (now a parish church) in Sallins, County Kildare where I spent many happy holidays with an uncle and aunt. Uncle George did the stations of the Cross with one knee on the bench. I think that Aunt Agnes disapproved of this and that it distracted her as she worked through her Rosary and litanies. Those Sallins stations made a deep impression on me: I remember shaking my fist at a 'baddie' who was maltreating the Lord: even still, now and again when visiting a church, I check to see if the station pictures are the same as those in Sallins. They are, I am happy to report, still there.

This simple church of Our Lady of the Rosary and the Guardian Angels has a newly-acquired treasure of local ancestral faith: a granite font from the ancient Bride's Church by the Liffey at Osberstown a mile away. It is hoped to dedicate it as the parish baptismal font.

I recall the lady of large build wearing a hat of Edwardian proportions who sailed grandly up the aisle and came to anchor in the front bench, thus reducing the liturgical participation of those directly behind her to hearing only. But the real duenna of the church was the sacristan-cum-caretaker whose bobs before the tabernacle in her to-ings and fro-ings were works of art and who, it was said, once presented the priest on Ash Wednesday with ashes hot from her own grate.

There was a choir gallery in a corner complete with harmonium. I have a recollection of the choir in action on First Fridays and of the gallery as a male enclave on Sundays dressed mainly, I would say, in navy blue: those were the days when male Ireland became elegantly navy blue on Sundays. I recall seating myself there but by that time I must have been a youth rather than a child to be allowed that dizzy distinction.

Mass was often said by Father P.J. Doyle. He was, I think, too 'upper-crust' to be really popular. He was, I'd say, genuinely anxious to widen the outlook of his congregation: I remember him giving his impressions of Nazism after a visit to Austria; and to raise their living standards: he lamented, with a devastating use of the plural, their ignorance of the various 'soups'. But whatever about being a lion in the pulpit, he was a lamb in the confessional: of that I had personal experience.

I have a memory of being cornered in the porch of Naas Church by a sister from the Mercy Convent next door and given a pamphlet on vocations to the priesthood (probably the famous one by Father Willie Doyle). Thank you, Sister, wherever you are. I have fleeting recollections of the old church in Caragh (now demolished) and the church attached to the Dominican college in Newbridge where my brother Billy was a boarder for a few years.

I was familiar with the ruined church at Bodenstown a mile from Sallins. (In medieval times the Knights Hospitaller of Kilmainham, Dublin had an 'income interest' in the church as they also had in Bride's Church at Osberstown). Many Sallins people, some of whom I knew, are interred in the adjoining cemetery. I was saddened and angered some years ago to find that some of the graves of plain people of Ireland, including that of a friend of mine, had been obliterated by being asphalted or concreted over for the convenience of those attending Wolfe Tone commemorations.

Not far from Bodenstown was the impressive Hiberno-Romanesque Church of Ireland church at Millicent with its high-heavenly dedication to Saint Michael and All the Angels and its distinctive lych-gate. Church, cemetery, gate, rectory and adjacent houses formed an Agatha Christie-like enclave on the banks of the Liffey.

School and University

Shortly after moving from Holy Faith to the Christian Brothers in Synge Street (where I stayed to the end of secondary school) I was confirmed in Saint Kevin's church next door: one of many confirmands with minds set on catechism questions and answers rather than on the Holy Spirit and the sacrament. I have a memory of people crowded at the back of the church – with mothers to the fore, I suppose. Prayer in Synge Street was much more in the classroom than in the church.

In 1937, full of the French Revolution and of chivalrous devotion to Marie Antoinette from the Leaving Certificate history course, I went with a friend, Philip Garrigan, on a Cook's tour to Paris. We visited the great basilica of the Sacred Heart that rises shining-white in Montmartre over the famous city. I remember the broad entrance steps, the crowds, the blaze of light around the exposed Blessed Sacrament. Against all the rules we climbed up a spiral stairs on to the roof. Right beside us the mighty bell or bells began to peal. Scared and deafened we spiralled down to be confronted by someone who looked like a policeman. His French was fluent and, I suspect, quite unchurchy. Our attendance at the fashionable Madeleine church was much more sedate.

I have some recollection of the baroque royal chapel at Versailles; but it could not compete with the grand staircase of the palace, which I peopled with the revolutionary mob coming to escort the royal family – 'the baker and the baker's wife and the baker's little boy', as they chanted – to Paris.

At University College, Dublin I met Father John Burke, one of the deans of residence (afterwards a war chaplain and bishop in India) who plied me with sandwiches in his house 84 on the Green and with spiritual direction in 86 where we held our Vincent de Paul meetings. I got to know the splendid university church that Newman built to the design of Hungerford Pollen and was so proud of ('the most beautiful church in the three kingdoms'): he dedicated it to Our Lady Seat of Wisdom and made it a Byzantine island in an archipelago of Georgian and Gothic. In all this perhaps we can see his dream of making his Catholic university a new Oxford, an intellectual centre for the English-speaking Catholic world.

The church was to symbolise 'the great principle of the university, the indissoluble union between philosophy and religion'. It was to play its part in forming the kind of laity he wanted: 'not arrogant, not rash in speech, not disputatious ... who know their religion, who enter into it, who know just where they stand, who know what they hold and what they do not, who know their creed so well that they can give an account of it, who know so much of history that they can defend it. I want an intelligent well-instructed laity.'

The fine bust of him by Sir Thomas Farrell was (and is) a reminder of the Newman legacy – though I rather regret that it does not have the words that Newman chose for his own memorial: 'Ex umbris et imaginibus in veritatem' ('Out of shadows and images into truth'). They are given, I am glad to say, in the Newman memorial in Dalkey church. I remember another reminder of Newman, this one in his pulpit, in the person of the famous Monsignor Ronald Knox whose life story was so like his. Newman's church is now appropriately a centre for the promotion of his beatification.

In my first university year I joined a group of Synge Street sixth-years for retreat in the Jesuit retreat house at Rathfarnham, Dublin. My main memory of the retreatants' chapel is having my undergraduate feathers ruffled by the Jesuit scholastic in charge of the hymns criticising my harmonium-playing. (Another scholastic, the delightful and affable Jack Hutchinson, and my lifelong friend Joe Veale, an organiser of the retreat, were to be confrères of mine years later in

Gonzaga). I remember looking at the scholastics and thinking with quite a touch of undergraduate uppishness, 'not for me'.

In the same year I paid a visit to the Cistercian abbey of Mound Melleray in County Waterford. I have no particular memory of the church there but I did come across a remarkable church-related item in the abbey museum: a set of dummy books which was really a penal-day tabernacle. You could picture a priest on the run using the book-case or a table against the book-case as an altar in front of the 'books' which were appropriately entitled '*De Nimia Dei Caritate*' ('Concerning the Superabundant Love of God'). It was rather like the screen-that-was-a-door but more eloquent and evocative.

A year later I visited Quarr Abbey in the Isle of Wight at the suggestion of Father Burke who had a plainsong bond with the monks there and thought I might become a Benedictine. I have a memory of the dim church, the monks singing the '*Salve Regina*' ('Hail, Holy Queen') after night prayer and the abbot moving through the church sprinkling us with holy water: *pax, pax, pax*. But not everyone was accepting the Benedictine peace. It was August 1939. A few weeks later the world, or a great part of it, was at war.

Simmonscourt

Poor Clare house in Dublin town
where prayer goes up and peace comes down
to heal the heart; and secular sounds
come in at times from the Horse Show grounds
My mother, bless her, loved those nuns
she'd get their prayers and bake them buns
they surely sensed, they surely knew
that she was good at praying too
I said the odd prayer there myself
had many a read at their pamphlet-shelf
and priested, *Deo gratias*
offered with them first holy Mass
Numen: a door, it seemed, of fire
hiding the Host that faced the choir
Portiuncula, cool and high
a chapel where I'd like to die

Grave of a Friend

Words on a shaded stone:
'This is my chosen resting-place':
Surely not a few feet of ground
nor trees and flowers and fields around
are dwelling enough for all that grace
that innocence, integrity
desire to love and serve as priest
to share with all God's joy and feast –
only in God eternally
Home Villas man is home

Sallins Three

Long overdue salute to three dear men:
George O'Hagan: summers sunshine-filled
dogs and gardens, engine in Leinster mills
childless, loving children, loved by them
he said his prayers, gently adopted me

Jim Shortall: memories of World War one
evenings of quiet chat in Sallins mill
hard to imagine him as one who killed
this gentle soldier from Portarlington
where now he rests, war over utterly

And Bony Rourke (we never called him 'John')
who died when he was young and I was small
someone to keep you smiling, I recall
he rests in Bodenstown: the grass is gone
his grave deleted by the powers that be

August 1939

Hail, holy Queen: we pray, are blessed
finale to the Compline hour
and so to rest
The peace of God envelops Quarr
but not the corridors of power
and so to war

2

FIRST JESUIT YEARS

Scholastic

In September 1940 I sat my B.A., was best man to my brother in the church of my baptism and joined the Society of Jesus. The novitiate was in Emo Court, a house originally designed by Gandon which had been the home of the earls of Portarlington. The salon and drawingroom had become the chapel: a place of Mass, prayer, vows and occasional hilarity. The novice-master Father John Neary (deftly portrayed by Benedict Kiely in *There was an Ancient House*) and his assistant Father Redmond Roche said Mass for us recollectedly and rubrically with no dramatics or folksiness whatsoever.

Father Frank Browne comes to mind here: Titanic passenger, chaplain in the first world war, parish missioner, famous photographer. He often said the Mass following the novices' Mass. We would hear the approaching squeak of the footwear that he used (much to our edification) only for Mass. He called them his 'Melchisedeks': bought, we were told, for his ordination. (In another version they had been worn by his fellow-chaplain, the heroic Father Willie Doyle who died in action). A kindly and charming man, he had a 'short fuse' and was prone to mingle fervent prayer with mild expletives when vestments were difficult to manage.

The evening mediation was done together in the chapel and could be a sleepy affair, especially in summer. There was the story of a novice who fell asleep with his book open at the chapter on the 'prayer of quiet'. The custom-book said that if you felt yourself dropping off you were to stand up: such was the heroic virtue we were expected to practise. The chapel had an idyllic situation, at least on a sunny day; great windows gave on to a lawn with its flowerbeds and Portarlington-era statues representing the four seasons (a novice, it was said, had once prayed before Winter under the impression that it was Saint Joseph) and down to a Portarlington-made lake.

I took my first vows in that chapel at Michaelmas 1942 and the following day departed, not for Rathfarnham as I had been to university, but in style by laundry-van for the philosophate at Rahan (Tullabeg), Offaly.

My rector there was Father Donal O'Sullivan who was deeply interested in liturgy and art. (He was entertainingly reported to have pyjamas of different colours to go with the liturgical seasons). He certainly preferred 'flowing' vestments to the then 'standard' more rigid Roman ensemble. He gave the community chapel a new sanctuary, a modern altar, a striking crucifix by Laurence Campbell and statues, also by Campbell, of Our Lady and (this was devotionally revolutionary) a young Saint Joseph. Most of all he enriched the chapel with a superb set of stained-glass windows by Evie Hone. (This major contribution to twentieth-century Irish art is now in a specially built chapel at Manresa House, Dublin). With all this and his emphasis on the Church as the Body of Christ he helped to prepare us for the changes of Vatican Two twenty years later.

Adjoining the house was the People's Church with its reredos painting of a refreshingly young Our Lady in her

Assumption, its tomb of Father John Cunningham the 'holy man' of Tullabeg tradition, its sombre panelling and spartan benches. It was frequented by local and not-so-local people: quiet reminders to the secluded students of the wider world without. Across the road were the thousand-year-old remains of the monastery originally founded by Saint Carthage in the sixth century, including a fragment with a notable rose window which had become part of a small Church of Ireland church. Further on were the Presentation convent and the parish church of Killina. The convent was founded in 1817; the church is from the Penal Days, predating 1788.

Further on still there was a Mass rock which, I am glad to say, is now the highlight of a garden dedicated to those who kept the faith here in penal times. The rock is inscribed 'IMS (Jesus, Magister, Salvator: Jesus, Master, Saviour) 1706'. The garden is landscaped with massive boulders symbolising defining moments and movements in Irish history.

To the north-west was Saint Patrick's chapel of ease of The Island where the saint chased the last snake in Ireland down a well and promptly made it a holy well. To the north-east, more historically, was Durrow of Colmcille with its great high cross. All in all an area rich in reminders of a long-held faith. I like to think that we absorbed some of this richness into our philosophical preoccupations.

Priest
And so to the ordination chapel of Milltown Park, Dublin on 31 July 1950. I remember my father in tears and the famous Archbishop John Charles McQuaid sacramentally imposing hands on us: no polite gentle contact this but a prolonged concentrated pressure that seemed to drive you into the ground. I think too of my nine confrères: seven Irishmen, the German Heinz Schulz who had fought not only for the Reich

but for his religious vocation and the Slovak Joseph Svec who had done forced labour during the Soviet advance into central Europe. The scene in the ordination chapel was much less festive on 11 February 1949 when Mass was said by the rector for a shattered community in various degrees of dress and undress after an early morning fire which had destroyed one wing of the house and taken the life of one young priest.

Special Masses followed ordination: in my old haunt the Poor Clare Convent in Ballsbridge; in the Holy Faith Convent of Haddington Road school; in the Sallins church of my early years; in Beechwood Avenue church for the Ballsbridge Bakery staff who had presented me with a chalice and paten; in the military chapel in Dublin Castle for my former Vincent de Paul confrères in university days. This last venue was indeed historic: the former Chapel Royal in what had been the heart of English/British rule in Ireland with its sumptuous woodwork still bedecked with coats-of-arms of centuries of viceroys, on the ground where Dermot O'Hurley, Margaret Ball, Francis Taylor, Oliver Plunkett, Peter Talbot and perhaps Peter Higgins had suffered for the faith.

In the Irish Jesuit system of the time newly-ordained priests combined their final year of theology with weekend pastoral work nearly always involving confessions and/or Mass or Masses in public churches. In these 'supplies', as they were called, we saw churches as places where we gave rather than received, as workshops rather than guestrooms: churches were the settings of our sacramental service of the people of God, where not only the glory dwelt but the grace was communicated, where we were in touch with people in a way never experienced before.

A few memories from that final year in Milltown. Two days after ordination I was in Dalkey church to hear my first confessions. I got to the confessional, instinctively opened the side door and then said to myself, 'You're in the middle this time'. The name on the confessional was that of a priest with a place in the history of the Church in Ireland and indeed in the world: Michael Creedon, confrère of the Servant of God Frank Duff in the beginnings of the Legion of Mary, part-author of its handbook, first spiritual director of its central council. A hard act to follow!

I remember going to Haddington Road for confessions at the end of October with Christ the King, All Saints and All Souls to be celebrated in a row and Bishop Dunne, successor to Bishop Wall, saying to us, 'It would be no harm to tell your penitents that one confession will do for all of them.' And I have memories of supplying for a priest who was a magician in his spare time and sleeping in a room furnished with the paraphernalia of his dread and exciting art; and of the consolation after a winter weekend in Enniskerry and Glencree of the enormous breakfast in the legendary McGuirk's Cottage at Lough Bray where they showed me a visitors' book that included the signature of Daniel O'Connell.

There were two supplies at Rathnew, County Wicklow: one in the church and one in a country house where the congregation or some of it lined the staircase. On one occasion Bessie the church sacristan (blessings on her) said to me, 'A very good young man prays here. He might become a priest. Talk to him.' I did and in due course he was ordained – but not in the Society of Jesus as I had hoped but in another religious order. He did splendid work in Nigeria and the United States. Any time I meet a member of that order I modestly tell him of all that they owe to me.

***

My father died seven months after my ordination. I owe him many things of course, including, I would say, my love of books:

I grew up surrounded by his second-hand acquisitions. (It was from him that I first learned of John Henry Newman). I especially remember his companionship in my later years at home. I think that he was delighted that I was getting the kind of education denied to him. He was a man of independent mind and great moral courage.Many years after my father's death I was thrilled to see his name on a GAA plaque in Wexford town commemorating the cup-winning Selskar Young Irelanders of 1893: one of the three Redmonds on the team. Appropriately the plaque is very near the remains of Selskar Abbey where Raymond le Gros Fitzgerald, ancestor of the Redmonds, was married.

★★★

After Milltown I went to Rathfarnham for 'tertianship' (Jesuitese for a process of spiritual renewal in preparation for final vows) with Irish and overseas companions. I brought one of these, a Chilean, to the Carmelite Church in Clarendon Street. It was a weekday; Mass was on. Rather like his forbears on a peak in Darien (according to the poet Keats) he looked at the large congregation and me with a wild surmise: 'Special feast-day?' I gave one of my best shrugs: 'Oh, no, this is usual.' I recall the remark attributed to Joseph Jungmann, probably the greatest liturgical scholar of the twentieth century, of a congregation (mostly poor people) in a Dublin church: 'These people have nothing to learn.'

I think it was at this time that I held the fort at Greenane, County Wicklow for a while and was only seconds away from a blunder of unimaginable proportions. I was just finishing the reading of marriage banns to a congregation when my angel guardian intervened in the nick of time to stop me from concluding with a flourish: 'May their souls ...'.

I spent the Lent of the tertianship at the Jesuit church in Gardiner Street, Dublin. A fine baroque church this with its superb ceiling, paintings of Jesuit history and beautiful chapels of the Sacred Heart and Our Lady of the Way. (The latter chapel has a very personal meaning for me: my mother prayed there every day while in the nearby Temple Street Hospital I fought for life at the age of six). It was a favourite church of the Venerable Matt Talbot: he used to kneel, I understand, towards the front of the right-hand transept near the sanctuary statue of the Sacred Heart. Since 1960 this church has housed the tomb of the Servant of God John Sullivan. I am told that for a short time he ministered here. Did these two special men ever meet? That Lent I celebrated Mass at the splendid high altar (no longer in use for Mass) which contains, it is said, stones from Nero's 'Golden House' (an interesting connection!). A special memory is seeing a tall black man doing the stations of the Cross on Good Friday. It was the first time I had seen a son of Africa saying his prayers and I was deeply moved. I also remember my fellow-tertian somehow getting lost in the wall of the church (!) – which in turn reminds me of a friend telling me years ago that a workmate of his was convinced that the Jesuit cellars in Gardiner Street were packed with gold.

Melchisedeks

They squeak along a corridor
negotiate a polished floor
they shuffle round the altar-space
and on occasion lose a lace

They speak of what it is to give
of what it is to really live
remind us of the Gift, the Feast
of what it is to be a priest

Rahan Mass-Rock

The yearning of the heart, the thrust of the mind
to reach full truth, leave shadowlands behind
the centuries of faith – all that's summed up
in 'Jesus, Master, Saviour': Word, Host, Cup

Jimmy Johnston

A private person as they say
not one to make a stir or fuss
prayed, studied, worked – industrious
one who preferred the quiet way

Pill to cope with sleeplessness
smoke and shouts at dawning day
thinks of convent Mass to say
half-awake delays to dress

Priest so briefly: God makes haste
priest forevermore: no waste

Ordination Day

Veni Creator, litanies, stretched-out flat
hands on your head, anointing, the Mass, the prayers
blessings, your father in tears, your mother's new hat
breakfast and family photographs: get more chairs
people come up to you, wish you all joy, then go
just a bit weary, not very much to say
how are the others, especially Heinz and Joe
thinking of loved ones dead or far away?

So many things, yet deep-down only one:
you are a priest: gift given, deed is done

3

GONZAGA YEARS

School

In 1952 I was appointed to teach in the newly opened Gonzaga College, Ranelagh, Dublin. For virtually all of my time there the community chapel was a converted dining room with windows giving a view of rockery, grass and trees. There were side-chapels here and there in the house: those were the days of one-celebrant Masses only: no concelebration. I often had the privilege of saying Mass with a penal-day chalice inscribed to the best of my memory: '*1685. P. Rodachan me fieri fecit*'.

I remember with appreciation those boys who came in to serve Mass, which was always in the morning: they were semi-indispensable because of the then strict rule about having a server. Let me include in my appreciation a devoted adult acolyte: Leonard Spollen, father of two of our pupils. I have a trivial memory of one boy combining his serving in the community chapel with pressing the Mass-bell into the mat to make circles. Perhaps he noticed my mannerisms and stored them in his sub-conscious: he is now a distinguished psychiatrist. Another trivial memory of the same chapel is learning my nickname through an open window: 'We call him

Toothpaste', a boy's voice floated in: this from my initials on the note for the prefect of studies if I thought a boy needed correction ('S.R. Toothpaste' was a popular brand).

Gonzaga developed and acquired a fine chapel. The architect was Andrew Devane who was to spend the last twenty-two years of his life working with Mother Teresa in Calcutta and becoming a Christian 'wisdom figure' to many who came his way. One memory of the chapel is quite harrowing: the boys singing a hymn I wrote, slightly changing one word into the name of a well-known person who was in public trouble at the time and with much emphasis and deplorable clarity making the name part of a text that neatly fitted the real-life situation.

One summer day I took time off from watching a tennis match in Sandymount between Gonzaga and another school and visited the nearby nineteenth-century Church of Ireland church of Saint John the Evangelist. It was modelled on a Norman church that Lady Pembroke had fallen in love with and had a High Church tradition. It was dignified and cool in its Romanesque stone. The notice board announced a Requiem Mass and May devotions. Part of the furnishing was a large picture of Our Lady and one of the books left out to help people to pray was by Pierre Charles, a French Jesuit. It was unarguably a place of blessing, of Christian prayer and to me, I hope, a lesson in ecumenism.

A visiting French priest asked me to show him a modern-style church. I brought him to Corpus Christi in Drumcondra, the most modern I could think of. He was not impressed – apparently we could not compete with Corbusier et al – and no doubt gave the dismissive shrug that the French are famous for. Then as we were leaving, God saved the honour of Dublin and Ireland by sending a garda along Griffith Avenue who saluted as he passed the church. Gallic gasp: 'le gendarme – fantastique!' – or words to that effect. My turn to shrug.

Not at all humorous was when a man came up to me, the only worshipper in Merrion Church, and told me that a voodoo curse or spell had been put on him and that he was worried out of his mind. I had never come across this particular nightmare – and there was no time to read it up! I wasn't exactly at my most adequate. I only hope that at least something of what I said helped him to trust the Lord of power and peace.

Ministries

For some of my time in Gonzaga I had a trickle of people for instruction in the faith and reception into the Church. One of these was a young Englishwoman called Dawn who had fallen in love with the first Irishman she met who had the rather different name of Patrick. She seemed to have an innate feeling for the faith. When I presented Our Lady's place in the Catholic system she said, 'Why do Catholics keep that lovely doctrine to themselves?' For her there was absolute baptism and no confession (she had certainly never been baptised) and Mass and communion in the community chapel in the presence of Patrick and friends: a touch of the Acts of the Apostles in a Dublin suburb, Easter Sunday, 1956. An Easter card still arrives every year.

Cyril also keeps in touch. He had been a Church of Ireland Sunday School teacher. His instruction was more difficult than Dawn's and at times, I'd say, quite exhausting for both of us. He became a good Catholic and was helped by the changes of Vatican Two. Thirty years later his son asked me to officiate at his marriage.

Then there was the young Muslim woman, in name a companion to Dawn (Rohiyah: 'Spirit of light'), whom I baptised in the Sacred Heart Convent in Leeson Street. The sister who instructed her had told me that every time she came she visited the Blessed Sacrament. After the baptism she slipped away. 'She's in the chapel', the sister said. And there we found her utterly absorbed, intent on One. A lesson for us all.

Finally in the list: Gerry. The church I associate with him is Saint Catherine's in Meath Street in the famous Liberties where I officiated at his marriage to Mary. The three of us were very nervous: we faltered and fumbled and foostered. I am eternally grateful to the local priest with whose help and encouragement we managed to achieve validity and liceity.

(On another occasion it was myself who kept a marriage ceremony 'on the rails'. I intervened to remind an elderly absent-minded parish priest that he had a marriage to officiate at after the gospel: he was proceeding straight on to the offertory. If the Mass had continued marriageless, the bride would surely have gone into hysterics: she had already been kept waiting by the groom and in her embarrassment had hidden in the adjoining cemetery).

Like many other Irish Jesuits engaged in teaching I gave retreats to religious communities in the holidays. I have a general memory of great kindness to me, of much prayer and work and of carefully maintained chapels that were clear expressions of faith and love focused on the Eucharist.

My first such retreat was to the Brigidines in Mountrath, Laois. Reading my office in the parish church one day, I got a lesson in prayer from the man a few benches in front of me. 'Put in a good word', he was saying again and again, probably to Our Lady.

During a retreat to Carmelites in Delgany, County Wicklow I turned around with the monstrance to give Benediction to the nuns and a few children to find a little black child with eyes opened wide in wonder at the Eucharist and its minister. I don't think I ever waved a monstrance with more fervour.

I remember in one retreat having to bring communion to a sick sister. A young sister was to escort me with candle and bell.

When I began to leave the altar she was at the door of the chapel. When I reached the door she was disappearing at the end of the corridor. And so on. I suppose I caught up with her in the sickroom. I was told afterwards that she had been admonished for walking too slowly, in danger of tripping up the priest. Clearly she had taken the admonition to heart. However, as a Jesuit remarked after an elaborate Tridentine High Mass in which priest, deacon and subdeacon had not been brilliant, 'No one got hurt!'

The convent I know best is that of the Sisters of Saint Joseph of Cluny at Gallen, Ferbane, Offaly. Over many years I have been generously welcomed there to give a retreat or Scripture course or simply to have a break. Gallen is indeed 'holy ground': one of those places where Christian continuity is almost palpably evident. The Cluny presence has been there for eighty years. Across the field on the verge of the river Brosna are the ruins of a medieval Augustinian priory. Nearer the house are millennium-old gravestones (one inscribed 'Or do Brolin') of a monastery on the site of a much older foundation by Canoc of Wales, close in time to Patrick.

When I went there first Gallen was full of novices and sisters. For many years the simple chapel was the prayer-place and vow-place of young women preparing for life in an institute that had quite a global mission. Years passed, vocations declined, Gallen grew quieter. You'd go into the chapel and find an elderly sister or two here and there in prayer: so hidden, so unobtrusive, so much part of this haven in the heart of Ireland. And then you'd discover that they had spent many years in places like Trinidad, Tahiti, the Seychelles, busy about the more important things in those sunny paradises of the tourist trail. These silent huddled figures before the tabernacle and the sanctuary light: that for me is a core memory of the chapel of Gallen.

Where the Mass was said

The Augustinian and Celtic remains at Gallen are only two of the 'bare ruined choirs' that I visited during the Gonzaga years. I think of my old haunt Bodenstown where a friend I was with flopped down on the grass saying, 'I like to pray wherever the Mass was said'.

I recall Clonmacnois, the once great monastic city on the Shannon, with its students from home and abroad, its writing of books and its praising of God; the superbly cloistered Franciscan friary of Askeaton, burial-place of Blesseds Bishop Patrick O'Hely and Father Con O Ruairc who died for the faith in 1579; and the Cistercian Bective (which the monks called 'Beatitudo Dei: The Blessedness of God') on the Boyne wherein lay most of the remains of its founder Hugh de Lacey, the formidable Norman Lord of Meath, until after gruesome litigation they were re-united with his head at Saint Thomas' Abbey in Dublin; and the Dominican priory in Sligo where contemporary coins were found, presumably hidden by departing friars in hope of an early return.

I climbed the tower of the Capuchin friary on the Hill of Slane and thought of the tradition of Patrick lighting the Easter fire that blazed in challenge across the Boyne to pagan Tara. At Tara I found a well and reflected: if Patrick did come to Tara (and he very probably did) and ministered there, this is surely the well he used for baptism. I blessed myself with its water with some sense, I hope, of an Irish Christian communion across fifteen centuries, with some understanding of what we had received and were being asked to pass on.

I officiated at several funerals at Mulhuddart, County Dublin where many of my mother's people are interred – so my memories of the place are understandably more 'family' than 'church'; but its ruined medieval church and ancient well of pilgrimage (both dedicated to Our Lady) speak of a tradition

of faith in which the family shared. It seems a far cry from a
ruined church in County Dublin to the majesty of Durhham
Cathedral where the remains of Cuthbert the great Anglo-
Saxon saint of northern England rest; but there may be a
connection. There is a tradition that Cuthbert was born in the
Clondalkin area south of the Liffey: his name seems to have
survived in 'Kilmahuddrick' near Clondalkin village.
Clondalkin monks may have brought his fame across the river:
'Mulhuddart' may mean 'Summit/Mound of Cuthbert'.

Ballintubber Abbey in Mayo is a happy exception to the
'Mass in the past tense' pattern: Mass has continued to be said
there with hardly a break for centuries since its suppression.
Father Egan, the man mainly responsible for its careful
restoration, gave a friend and myself the story and a conducted
tour in 1968. Nearby is a remarkable Mother and Child by
Heckner: Our Lady not looking down at her Son at her breast
but holding him high, showing him strongly, challengingly as if
to say, 'This is the One who matters, the One you need'. It is a
presentation in keeping with a place where the Mass refused to
die.

London

In 1955 I visited London. From Westminster Abbey I remember
the dark and high tomb of King-Saint Edward the Confessor,
once a great pilgrimage shrine; and the flat-topped tomb of
Chaucer: a Catholic tomb usable as an altar for Mass. I took
part in a pilgrimage in honour of 'the man for all seasons', Saint
Thomas More. We went by the Thames, the river that was a
main-street in his life: from Chelsea where he lived via Lambeth
where he refused an oath that involved denying papal authority
and Westminster where he was tried to the Tower of London
where we visited the cell in which he was imprisoned. We
ended our pilgrimage in a church he had frequented.

On another visit to the Tower I was 'confronted' and indeed challenged over the centuries by the fourteen times tortured and now canonised martyr Henry Walpole through a rough cross and inscription cut into the wall, naming him as a priest of the Society of Jesus.

I recall Warwick Street church, favoured for fashionable weddings with brides bestowing their bouquets on Our Lady and discreetly visited, it was said, by Queen Mary, wife of George V. It was once the chapel of the Portuguese Embassy, later of the Bavarian Embassy, one of those places with diplomatic immunity where penal-day London Catholics, by courtesy of the foreign power, could attend Mass.

In Saint Etheldreda's Church I thought of Douglas Hyde's memoir of it: editor of the communist *Daily Worker*, he went in, his mind in turmoil, noticed that two little girls came from Our Lady's shrine looking very happy, went to the shrine himself and prayed, his prayer the title of a Gershwin song: 'Lady, be good (to me)'. She was: he and his wife became Catholics.

A special delight of the London visit was a great Italian celebration in Soho for the feast-day of Our Lady of Mount Carmel: Mass in Saint Patrick's (that day I suppose it was San Patricio's) and a joyous street procession. As I approached people clapped: Cardinal Griffin was just behind me.

Belgium

In the 1960s I went on pilgrimage with groups to Banneux in eastern Belgium three times. A young girl, Mariette Beco, had reported apparitions of Our Lady under the title of 'Virgin of the Poor' with a message 'for all nations'. The pilgrim area in the beautiful Ardennes had been developed with discretion: we were told that when some people had wanted to build a basilica, Mariette pointed out that Our Lady had asked only for a little chapel. One Mass after another was celebrated in the chapel: you booked your 'slot'. My devotion was badly dented by my protracted struggle to open the tabernacle with people waiting for communion and a priest in the wings doubtless struggling with impatient thoughts.

On one occasion I had to preach to a general congregation. I decided (tactful me!) not to mention Irish missionaries in that part of Europe so as not to offend national sensibilities. After the Mass a priest (I think he was a Belgian) complained: 'Why didn't you mention that it was the Irish who brought the faith here?' You can't win!

I remember watching the pilgrim crowds from Belgium and other countries – including Germany – on Assumption Day and noting the friendly and helpful atmosphere. I reflected that recently enough many of these pilgrims had been 'officially' enemies during the Second World War (there had been fierce fighting in the Banneux area): how inhuman, how 'artificial' war was.

One excursion took us to Aachen and I gazed with some awe at the massive tomb of Charlemagne, that mega-figure in the history of Europe. Our visit to the United States war cemetery near Liège was a sombre experience: the rows and rows of graves with crosses for Christians and stars of David for Jews; the austere colonnade inscribed with the names of the American fallen (including with poignant irony German names); at one end of the colonnade a campaign room and at the other a meditation room with a semi-poetical prayer by John Henry Newman cut shiningly into the wall. To someone with religious faith the cemetery was a vast church of the dead and an invitation to prayer.

Our group was entertained by the Countess de Theux, a relative of the King of the Belgians, at her chateau, part of which had been occupied by both Germans and Americans during the Second World War. I visited the chateau chapel with its atmosphere of ancestral faith focused on the Eucharist in a part of Europe that had experienced more than one tidal wave of turmoil and trauma.

Italy

'Go to Rome and Florence', said Father Provincial at his most benevolent, 'it will do the history good.' (I was teaching history at Gonzaga). Rome is of course a great place for churches and chapels and I had a field day – or rather a field three weeks – there in June and July 1967.

The Sistine Chapel where the Popes are elected is very special. It is dominated by the work of Michelangelo, including the fearsome Last Judgement and the profound, finger-touching God and Adam in the instant of creation. Art like this demands full attention, which is difficult when you are in a surging crowd with camera bulbs flashing against all the rules and the protests of chapel staff.

Very different was the atmosphere in the Blessed Sacrament Chapel of Saint Peter's: in the main part of the basilica the hum of the crowd: here silence and for the man I saw there the silence of adoration: in this he was like Rohiyah in the Leeson Street Convent.

I give some 'Jesuit' moments. I visited the basilica of Saint Paul Outside-the-Walls where Ignatius and some of his companions took their first vows as Jesuits. I said Mass in one of the two rooms where he spent the last years of his life, prayed (at least I hope I did) in the roof-garden where he prayed, at times in tears of consolation, and paid my respects at his resplendent altar-tomb in the great Church of the Gesu.

I visited the rooms of Aloysius Gonzaga who renounced a 'life in the purple' in his quest for God; and the tomb in the exquisite Church of San Andrea-in-Quirinale of the teenage Polish aristocrat Stanislaus Kostka who travelled from Vienna to Rome to enter the novitiate where he died. Andrea Pozzo, Jesuit brother and baroque painter, travelled in the opposite direction, from Italy to Vienna. I marvelled at his masterpiece of a ceiling in the Church of Saint Ignatius: a three-dimensional depiction of the saint's ascent into heaven.

Directly beneath the medieval basilica of San Clemente is a remarkable example of a place where the Mass was once said: a fourth century basilica, dating from the time when the Roman State gave freedom to the Church. As though symbolising the historical watershed, a tombstone in the basilica has a beautifully incised pagan inscription on one side and a crudely done Christian inscription on the other; and annexed to the church on a lower level are the remains of a Mithraeum: a temple of Mithra, the pagan deity honoured especially by soldiers; and beneath that runs a stream that connects with the Colosseum.

San Clemente brought the early Church graphically to mind, as did the Mamertine prison where according to tradition Saint Peter was detained before his martyrdom in the persecution of Nero. My special 'Peter' moment came when I stood at the excavated space which is accepted as where he was interred when Nero was done with him. It is directly underneath the high altar of Saint Peter's where his successor celebrates Mass on great ceremonial occasions in a bi-millennial continuity and communion.

The wealthy aristocrat who was to become Pope Gregory the Great turned his family home on the Coelian Hill into a monastery dedicated to Saint Andrew. When he was Pope he sent its prior Augustine and a party of its monks to preach the Gospel in what had been Roman-ruled Britannia. I read and photographed an inscription commemorative in part of the link between Saint Andrew's and the Anglo-Saxons. There is quite a waft of England on the Coelian.

I got a waft of Ireland in San Clemente where Irish Dominicans have been for centuries. But my real 'Irish' moment was in San Pietro-in-Montorio when my guide pulled the carpet back and I saw the grave of Hugh 'the Great O'Neill' and beside it that of his son: graves that evoke echoes and images of Kinsale and Dunboy and the Flight of the Earls, of the watershed of a nation and the collapse of a culture – but happily not its death.

Quietest of all Roman basilicas is that of Saint John of the Latin Gate on the site where according to rather dubious tradition the apostle suffered in the time of the emperor Domitian. No renaissance splendour or baroque exuberance here: rather the dim serenity of the Romanesque going back for a thousand years. There I was, soaking in the centuries, when the organist came out to practise. I prepared for music that would promote the soaking. What I got was Tchaikovsky's 'Dance of the Sugar-Plum Fairy' from the 'Nutcracker' suite, played with a few wrong notes.

I visited the adoration chapel in a wing of the Palazzo Venezia. It was Marie Reparatrice of Merrion Square and Sacré Coeur of Montmartre all over again: the same Lord, the same presence, the same faith. In the Fascist era the Palazzo was Mussolini's headquarters: at times adorers prayed to the background of his speeches from the balcony and applause of the crowd in the piazza. Let us hope that their prayers reached him at the hour of his appalling death.

While in Rome I stayed at the Collegio Bellarmino. I noted with interest that the nearby café or trattoria was called, perhaps in deference to its ecclesiastical neighbours (and patrons?), 'La Sagristia'. After three wonderful weeks I said good-bye to my hosts and faced north.

I arrived in Assisi tired and hungry and mudstained (I had fallen into a ditch the previous night – but that's another story),

feeling that no Franciscan had come there as poor as this Jesuit.
I did what I had come to do: said Mass at the tomb of Francis.
The saint's remains are in a stone coffin inset at a height into a
great broad pillar in the centre of the lower church of the
basilica. I said Mass at one of the four small altars at the base of
the pillar. My server was a Franciscan brother who kept
working at his table, interjecting 'et cum spiritu, Amen' and so on
from time to time. I'm not sure if he rang a bell. The mode of
serving would have raised eyebrows in Dublin, but it seemed all
right in Assisi. I visited San Damiano, the church of Francis'
conversion experience, and in the convent named after her
looked (rather gingerly) at the remains of Saint Clare.

Finally Florence: one of the great treasure-cities of the
world in architecture, sculpture and painting: the divine
Florence, as it has been called. You could say that for two and a
half centuries (from the late thirteenth to the early sixteenth) it
was the home of the leading artists of Europe. And so much of
the art is associated with the faith and is found in churches.

One of Michelangelo's last Pietàs (many would say his
greatest) is that of the Florence Duomo (cathedral). I gather
that the Pietà I found in the Duomo itself is a copy, the original
being in the more protected setting of the Duomo Museum.
The Nicodemus (or perhaps Joseph of Arimathea) figure,
generally accepted as a self-portrait of Michelangelo, supports
the Christus and helps Our Lady to hold him. While the Lord's
face is at peace, the body is exhausted and broken. This
masterpiece of great tenderness can be taken to embody
Michelangelo's faith in Christ and his own preparation for
death: for some time he intended it for his own tomb.

In the former Dominican priory of San Marco I found the
delicate and mystical frescoes of Fra Angelico (the
Annunciation is the most loved) and the mementoes of its best-
known (and to many its martyred) prior Savonarola. I looked at

the graceful campanile of the Duomo, designed by Giotto who also supervised the first stages of its construction: 'Giotto's tower', wrote Longfellow, 'the lily of Florence blossoming into stone'. (The red Turk's Cap lily is the heraldic sign of this unique city). And I wondered at the breath-taking reliefs of Ghiberti on the east door of the Duomo baptistery. In a salute to one genius by another, Michelangelo said that it deserved to be the door of Paradise.

***

The doors of God opened and shut quite often for the extended Redmond family during my time in Gonzaga: uncles, aunts and cousins took their leave; as in the immediate family did my mother and sister. My mother, whose prayers and example had done so much for me (and indeed for many others: by nature and grace she was a 'giver') died in 1966. She had spent her last years in Dalkey, so her funeral was from the church where I had heard my first confessions and said my first parish Mass. My sister Moira, the eldest child of my father's first marriage, died in 1970 in New York where she had spent most of her life. You could almost say that she died saying 'Jesus' and 'Mary': she was found with her Rosary beads in her hands. I received the news of her death while giving a retreat in the Marie Reparatrice Convent in Merrion Square where she had attended Mass at the time of my ordination twenty years before.

***

Chalice
Sixteen-eighty-five: a year or two
of royal favour for the likes of you
then Boyne and Limerick, penal-night again
did you ever feel the Mass-rock rain?
and Father Rodachan who had you made:
who was this man who studied, worked and prayed
to keep the faith alive, who held you up
the symbol of his life, his Jesus-cup?
passed on from hand to hand, from priest to priest
from Mass to Mass: always the Gift, the Feast
from rock to house, from house to church you move
while over you are said the words of love

And now I hold you, say the words, adore
and pray for all who've held you thus before

Light
Rohiyah (Spirit of light) and Dawn
women who shared a primordial name
echoing Genesis, echoing John
women from different worlds they came
to Him who said, 'I am the light
I am the way, come, follow me
leave the shadows, leave the night
share my day eternally'

Gallen

Canoc comes here, makes the place
an outpost oasis of Christ
south of the Riada line
changes the bread and the wine
into Him sacrificed

Others come here, live in grace
Eucharist: come and be fed
others prefer death and sin
captains and kings, battle-din
meadows and Brosna are red

Then there's a church by the stream
the sons of Augustine arrive
preach his Confessions, his word
'You are all made for the Lord
only in Him you're alive'

Sisters appear with their dream
'This is the place where we start
to hope in Him day after day
to make Him our life and our way
to live evermore in his Heart'

Thomas More

Sweet Thames! Run softly, softly run
from dawn to noon, to setting sun
from day to year, from youth to age
you've been my river, scene and stage
whereon I've acted out my play
until this hour, this Lambeth day
Sweet Thames! Run softly, softly run
praise God with me: the field is won

Stanislaus Kostka

San Andrea: honey-coloured walls
across the altar-tomb the sunlight falls
what's left of Stanislaus on earth is there
I click my camera and say a prayer

Poland, Vienna, Dillingen and Rome
he presses on, he seeks his real home
the innocence and grace – all that's elsewhere
forget your camera, just say your prayer

Pietà

Four figures: the Christ
dead, sacrificed
is this the end?
Nicodemus the friend
who came by night
now where's the light?
face laid to face
the Full of grace
still mothers Him
and Magdalen
keeps wondering why
her Love should die

4

AFRICA YEARS

Xavier House, Saint Ignatius' Church & 'The Stony Place'
I went to Zambia in 1971 to teach in the newly-built Jesuit
novitiate (named Xavier House while I was there) in Lusaka:
which meant among other things a new sequence of churches
and chapels. The first of these was of course the novitiate
chapel with its Picassoesque mural by Father Brendan Duddy. I
recall the lively singing of the novices from various parts of
English-speaking Africa (especially their singing of my own
pieces) and at least one historic occasion: the first vows of
Groum Tesfaye: so far as I know the first Ethiopian to take
vows in the Society of Jesus: a long-term fruit of an apostolic
contact that began in the sixteenth century.

Earlier in this book I mentioned the 'African apparition' in
Delgany, County Wicklow. I met smaller editions of it in
Zambian churches on their mothers' backs as the mothers
received communion and (in one case) while the mother was
being baptised. A larger edition was my friend Clement in Saint
Ignatius' Church, one of the Jesuit churches in Lusaka. I did
some weekend work there, including providing the music at
weddings. Clement was only too happy to be an unofficial

witness and to sit beside me at the organ, urging me to play louder.

The marriage homilies that stay with me are those of a Zambian priest and an Irish priest (other than the parish priest whose homily I knew by heart). The Zambian, who could speak more candidly than an expatriate priest could, warned the couple in front of their extended families (the extended family is very important in African society) not to let their relatives interfere with their marriage: family intrusion had ruined many a marriage. The Irishman said that he visited two kinds of homes: after visiting one kind he would give thanks that he had never married; after visiting the other kind he regretted that he had not married. He wished the couple the second kind.

One of my greatest consolations in Zambia was giving communion in Saint Ignatius': the people of different colours and cultures presenting themselves at the same altar: black, white, brown, African, European, Indian. You got a sense of the one Christ for all nations, of what the Catholic Church really means. You felt an impatience with unthought-out prejudices that sometimes disfigure even 'religious' people.

But there was one person (an Indian woman) to whom I did not give communion. When I came to her the Mass-server, more knowledgeable than I, shook his head and motioned me past her. I gathered that she was not a Christian and somewhat mentally disturbed. When the rest of us had received, she sang a rather long song with quiet devotion, tinkling a little bell. It was moving and beautiful and more than a little sad. But the Lord who is not bound by his sacraments was with her, I'm sure.

In contrast to the spacious well-furnished Saint Ignatius' was the thatched mud building with rough-hewn benches that I saw near Namwala ('The Stony Place') in southern Zambia.

Plainest of the plain, but a work of faith and love by the smiling man who proudly gave the parish priest and myself a conducted tour. At that time Mass had not been celebrated there but people, I'd say, had begun to use it for prayer. It was a moving 'surprise of the faith' for me.

Song and Dance

Another moving (in another sense) experience was the dancing at Mass at the Gloria and the presentation of the gifts: part of the development of an African liturgy. A surprise for my Irish ears was all the singing at Mass, nearly always in a lively tempo which most Irish people would find strange in worship, with the drum as the main accompaniment. This instrument is the musical epitome of Africa: a rhythm-world largely secret to those who are not African. In time, please God, it will be the musical symbol of Africa's faith in the Lord.

My most striking experience of the liturgical drum was at a Mass of religious commitment in Lusaka. As the procession moved into the church there was none of the usual rhythmic singing: only a strong drumbeat repeated at regular intervals. This was the traditional signal of the approach of the chief – the chief on this occasion being the Archbishop of Lusaka. 'At last, Redmond', I told myself, 'you're taking part in a Grand Entrance!'

But my biggest church surprise in the line of music was when I celebrated the Easter Night liturgy with a Cork priest (the Corkonians are everywhere!) and his parish of poor people on the edge of Ndola, one of the largest cities in Zambia. He asked me to sing the proclamation of the Resurrection, the Exultet, in Latin as he had no vernacular chant for it and he thought that the people would prefer something sung to something said. We began the celebration with a mobile Passion Play around the church grounds with car headlights helping to illuminate the scene. Then we lit the Easter candle and packed (really packed) into the simple church and I began the Exultet. I expected to have to sing the responses that come one-third way through. Surprise, surprise! Back came the responses perfect in note and roof-lifting in volume: *'Et cum spiritu tuo, Habemus ad Dominum, Dignum et justum est'*. So when my 'progressive' friends tell me that Latin is dead in the Church, I smile serenely, thinking of an Easter Night among poor people in Central Africa.

Cathedrals

I recall a remarkable address by President Kenneth Kuanda of Zambia in the Catholic cathedral in Lusaka after a memorial Mass for Father Patrick Walsh of the Society of Jesus. Father Walsh was one of the first Irish Jesuits to work in what was then Northern Rhodesia and he became a personal friend of Kaunda, leader of the independence movement. In due course Northern Rhodesia became Zambia, Kaunda became President and Father Walsh helped to get the Irish government interested in helping the new state. But saddened by the legalising of abortion and, as he saw it, the widening gap between rich and poor, he left Zambia for health reasons and died in, of all places, apartheid South Africa as the guest of the papal representative there.

Half in tears, Kaunda addressed Father Walsh 'I promise you that while I am president the rich will not get richer and the poor poorer.' (Shortly afterwards he announced a programme of reform). Outside the church people crowded around him. I remember looking at his broad back and thinking how vulnerable he was at that moment to an assassin's attack.

There is an imposing Anglican cathedral in Lusaka, modelled, I was told, on the famous post-war cathedral in Coventry. It was considered 'High Church'. I recall being at its crowded carol service, which was quite an event in the Lusaka religious calendar; and the marriage there of a Catholic and a non-Anglican Protestant with the officiant a Jesuit confrere of mine and myself the organist: quite an interesting blend of persons and place. But my major memory of that church is taking part with the novices in a production of Malcolm Williamson's opera *The Red Sea*. We were the defeated and drowned Egyptian army and we had to collapse on the floor while delightful children, representing waves, danced over us. I remember saying to myself at that dramatic moment, 'there was a lot implicit in those vows you took'.

Kasisi

Kasisi near Lusaka has had a Catholic presence for nearly a century. I was saying Mass there one day and had just read the gospel about the Lord healing the blind Bartimaeus of Jericho when the door opened and a blind man came in and groped his way to a seat. I thought: if only I could do what He had done. It was like the Lord teaching me a lesson about my own inadequacy in contrast to his power. I think I was conscious of Bartimaeus of Kasisi for the rest of the Mass. It was a humbling experience for me: at least I hope that it was.

My other church experience in Kasisi was more relaxed. One Christmas-time I saw some children assembled to see the crib move. (I gather that it was a special request programme). Lights went on, machinery whirred, Our Lady bowed, Saint Joseph waved his staff, the Baby blessed. Sophisticates may smile, scholars shudder, artists shake their heads. The essence was authentic: the children were meeting the Child.

Picture-Book

Some quick pictures from my Zambian church-memory album: Palm Sunday procession along the roads adjacent to

Saint Ignatius' church with a police escort probably supplied by the Minister of Home Affairs who was a member of the congregation; Mass with the Poor Clares who announced their convent as a 'house of prayer for all the nations' (Isaiah 56,7) and like our novices were much given to singing but rather more lyrically; Easter Night liturgy with the Daughters of the Redeemer, a sisterhood founded by Archbishop Milingo of Lusaka, and with some unbaptised neighbours; Mass for students in a lecture-hall of the university; retreat for students of Saint Charles Lwanga Teacher Training College in the fine church which Father Sean McCarron made the centrepiece of the campus he designed; the tower (kept as a memorial) of the church built at Chikuni by Father Joseph Moreau, founder of the Jesuit mission in the future Zambia.

All this and much more in the context of a young Church (with a new hierarchy almost completely Zambian) coping with Vatican Two changes and of a tribal people recently a colony and protectorate and now a state poised between the United States-led west and the Communist bloc.

Churches of Hope

One day a few young men came to the novitiate looking for a priest who would say Mass at an agricultural centre about twelve miles away, even just once a month. I said that I would come twice a month but that I could not drive a car. They said that they would collect me and bring me back. And so for quite a period we had Mass in English and Chichewa in a rather primitive classroom with the teacher's table for an altar, the mothers with their babies, one of the young men translating my homily into Chichewa and a collection to pay for the petrol. One Sunday we had the baptism of a baby. It was a wonderful example of lay action and of esteem for the Mass that we could learn from. The period ended when the petrol dried up because of rationing.

A rather similar experience was celebrating Mass in a psychiatric hospital: how avidly these poor people received the bread of life. It was like a crowd scene in the gospel of Mark: the pressing around the Great Healer.

Adam (now Cardinal) Koslowiecki, former prisoner of the Nazis in Dachau and retired first archbishop of Lusaka, asked me to give a retreat to teachers and catechists at his mission of Chingombe in central Zambia. It was heart-warming to see and hear these men, led by the local chief, at their prayers: they reminded me of 'traditional' Irishmen who took their faith seriously – except that they sang far more.

And faith was linked with a dignified formality. Dissatisfied with my handshake for each of them after the last retreat talk, the chief said to me, 'We are not like chickens that run away. We want to say goodbye properly.' So next morning we stood in a circle in the August sunshine and the chief in his red and black House of Chiefs gown read his speech of thanks, calling me their 'father in God'; and these men of modest means presented their token of appreciation. The Chingombe experience was a highlight of my time in Zambia. A retreat card in my breviary reminds me to pray for my 'children'.

A moving Chingombe memory is the Zambian flag at half-mast outside the school in this remote corner of Africa in mourning for Pope Paul VI who had just died. I like to think that this was more than a formal gesture but was a 'thank you' for his appeal for justice and generosity towards the 'majority world' in his social encyclical 'The Progress of Peoples'.

I remember the time that Bishop James Corboy of Monze in Southern Zambia and I went to visit some sisters who managed two clinics in an area caught up in the troubles on the Zambia-Rhodesia border. The Zambian soldiers we met could not have been more friendly; and the bishop said that the friendliness was due to the sisters who remained to care for the people despite the danger. We had lunch with two of the sisters in the thatched mud building where there was Mass once a month. At one end was the altar, in the centre rough benches, at the door-end the 'dinette'. The sisters were Maltese and Indian, the people in the area were Zambian and Zimbabwean, the bishop and I were Irish: quite an international confluence.

Father Bill Lee was a confrère and friend of mine in Gonzaga. Before coming there he had worked in the then Northern Rhodesia and had founded a mission at Kasiya in the south of the territory. About twenty years later I stood at a few mounds of mud pointed out to me as the remains of the simple church he had built: perhaps it had been his hut or a combination of church and living space. Here or hereabouts had been the first home of the Eucharistic Christ in this part of the world: a flag of faith had been raised and a position secured. Praise the Lord and thank you, Bill.

Kenya

Nearly all my time in Africa was spent in Zambia. I was in Malawi for a few hours (that hardly counts) and in Kenya a few times. I visited more than once the grave of that Envoy Extraordinary of the Legion of Mary, the Venerable Edel Quinn, in a missionaries' cemetery in Msongari, a suburb of Nairobi. I have some recollection of the modern Catholic cathedral in Nairobi. But my enduring Kenyan church-memory is of a small church in the Rift Valley north of Nairobi. It was build by homesick Italian prisoners in the East African theatre of the Second World War. There it is, a little part of Italy in the Kenyan Highlands, overlooking that awesome dent in the planet where perhaps the human race began.

***

One day in 1978 my rector gently told me that word had come from Dublin that my brother Billy had died. One could not have asked for a better brother. I remember his concern for me, his interest in my dithery desire to be a priest. In later years he was always ready to 'give a hand'. He had a great sense of humour and of discipline. Like his father he had lots of moral courage; unlike him he had a passion for jazz, playing everything in the key of E.

***

Communion in Saint Ignatius' Church, Lusaka
Faces black and brown and tan and white
come to share one Bread
theirs one radiant Light
'the queen of colours', as Augustine said

Behind each face ancestral memories:
cricket-bats, hurleys, drums
islands in summer seas
welcome from half the world to Him who comes

I move along, I'm learning quite a bit:
the Food, the love, the Body – this is it:
Ecclesia
Catholica

Love
All that mud
all that wood
build and hew
loving You

All that blood
cross of wood
I worked too
loving you

Bartimaeus of Kasisi

The scene of the gospel was Jericho town
the man who was blind they couldn't keep down
he shouted for sight
suddenly light
with eyes seeing Him

I'd just finished reading – he opened the door
groped to a seat, stick tapping the floor
I groaned in my mind:
'I can't heal the blind
not being Him'

I felt – well, inadequate; Mass went ahead
I prayed, consecrated, gave out living Bread
ever aware
of blank eyes astare
with the heart seeing Him

Easter Night
A hill reminding me of Slane
but here no Boyne flows by
the tropic air is still and dry
without a fight with wind and rain
the candle's lit; across the plain
Christ in symbol glows and burns
'I'm the goal of all that yearns
lift your hearts, I live again'

'This is the night': black faces shine
novices praise the risen Lord
speak the strong prophetic word
bring the bread and bring the wine
others are there: some eight or nine
all unbaptised, a family
still groping in simplicity
to find the Lord in Easter sign

I'm told they like to come and pray
and sing a song and beat a drum
You said the children were to come
well, here they are – don't let them stray
(anonymous Christians, we could say)
communion for us but not for them
but I wish them the joy of Bethlehem
of the Supper-room, of Easter day

The alleluias end, the air is still
the novices wish me joy and say goodnight
I say a prayer and then blow out the light
the anonymous Christians vanish down the hill

Grave of an Envoy
The grass, the trees
Nairobi graves of missionaries
Edel: so many memories:
the grace and charm, assignments done
all for a Lady and her Son
– and then They come

The Church in the Rift Valley
Small brown men from Italy
captured in the tide of war
by the cooler Englishry
built this road in Africa

Lonely men, they dreamt of home
of noonday towns and hills of vine
Palermo, Naples, Florence, Rome
of opera and evening wine

They build the sort of church they knew
from floor to roof Italian-styled
with high-enthroned in blazing hue
Santa Maria and her Child

And there they went to Mass and prayer
while guards discreetly stood around
and through the Kenyan mountain air
they made a brave Italian sound

At last the soldiers went away
the wave of freedom rolled along
and now still browner people pray
and fill the church with Kenyan song

Mother and Child still guard the Rift
gaze on the mountains, scan the sky
as though they saw the primal drift
of hominids from Olduvai

5

LATER YEARS

I returned to Ireland in 1980 and joined the Jesuit community in John Austin House on the North Circular Road, Dublin. The house is named after an eighteenth-century Dublin Jesuit of the later penal days who, as well as doing parish work, devoted himself to the education of boys. After the suppression of the Society of Jesus he became a priest of the archdiocese. His grave is in Saint Kevin's Park near Camden Street close to that of Blessed Dermot O'Hurley the martyred archbishop of Cashel. As regards church-haunting in these later years, it has been a time of re-visiting familiar places and opening new doors.

'Dub' Churches
By 'Dub' church I mean a church whose congregation is steeped in the way of life of poorer Dublin people. Perhaps those who think that a too-narrow description will accept it as a sort of pragmatic shorthand: I'm not a sociologist! There are of course many such churches: the four given here are simply a personal preference.

Saint Michan's, Halston Street, named after the patron saint of this part of Dublin (he was probably a tenth or eleventh century Dublin-Norseman), is the successor of a nearby penal-day church and is the proud possessor of its holy water font. It also possesses a notable window depicting the fifteen mysteries of the Rosary. It has an atmosphere of quiet dignity in keeping with its history as a focus of Catholic faith in this area for nearly two centuries. Its special devotional tradition is the Novena of Grace in honour of Saint Francis Xavier, dating back to a penal-day Jesuit connection. I remember ending the novena there with a blessing given with a crucifix reputedly used by the saint and holding it with great care because of its fragility.

The crucifix is kept in the next-door Presentation Convent, which shares in the aforesaid venerable connection. The stones of the Calvary rockery almost in front of the convent are from the penal-day church.

Shortly before going to Zambia I was at a Mass in the Capuchin church in Church Street for those involved in or aspiring to missionary work in that country. Now I go there for evening Mass. Its architect was J.J. McCarthy, 'the Irish Pugin', and its decorated Gothic style is in keeping with its lyrical name of Saint Mary of the Angels. It was opened in 1891 but there was a Capuchin presence in this part of Dublin for nearly two centuries before that.

I have very positive memories of an Ethiopian member of the church staff celebrating Mass. It was delightful to see how this man from a distant culture was accepted by the deeply 'Dub' congregation. Sign of the times! – and of the future? Certainly a sign of the *Catholic* Church. The Jesuit John Sullivan used to pray here at the shrine of Saint Anthony: he had thought of being a Capuchin and never lost his love for the Franciscan ideal. Two Church Street priests attended the 1916 leaders before their execution, surely praying that flights of angels would sing them to their rest.

Another church dedicated to Our Lady and that I frequent for evening Mass is on City Quay in the south dockland. It is an unpretentious church, traditionally associated of course with the docker community, looking across the Liffey at the rather less unpretentious Financial Centre and the Gandon grandeur of the Custom House. With its statues and shrines it is 'traditional'; with its excellent lay readers and weekly evening prayer of the Church it is of Vatican Two. Near the church beside the bridge named after him is an evocative sculpture by James Power of that renowned 'Dub', the Venerable Matt Talbot.

I move along the waterfront to Ringsend, one of the most 'characterful' parts of Dublin. (There are some Ringsenders, no doubt, who would insist that Ringsend is distinct from and older than Dublin, the latter being a sort of suburb that got out of control). It is surely a historical irony that a Catholic church should be at or very near the arrival-point in 1649 of Oliver Cromwell who said that while he interfered with no one's conscience he would not allow the Mass in any place under his rule. But there it is, Saint Patrick's in neo-Gothic, suitably spired and (very unusual for a Dublin Catholic church) boasting a chiming tower clock; unusual too in having a shrine of Saint Martha.

I remember many years ago meeting a Ringsend man and remarking on his name which was strange to me. 'That's a Cornish name', he said: in the old days the fishing link between Ringsend and ports in Cornwall (and doubtless in other parts of Britain) let to intermarriage. Certainly many of the names memorialised in Saint Patrick's have an overseas sound: Bailman, Bissett, Canterbury, Dixon, FitzHarris, Jevens, Lovely, Lowes, Mann, Memery, Nelson, Royal, Sims, Teidt, Waddock, Worthington ... They catch the eye; as does the bench-plate inscription that asks for prayers for the most forgotten priest in Purgatory.

Special Churches and Chapels

While I was assistant archivist of the Irish Jesuit province I received in gift the frayed and faded green maniple of Father Willie Doyle, the heroic chaplain who died in action in the First World War (the maniple was the vestment priests used to wear on the forearm). One of his men, Tom Dalton, took possession of it with the permission of his commanding officer. His daughter Pauline and her cousin Maureen Giles kindly gave it to us. It evokes thoughts of the unusual 'churches' and 'chapels' in which it was used: a hospital ward, a barracks-room, a Flanders field, a dugout – often with the congregation in imminent danger of death. In one letter Father Willie describes saying Mass on a biscuit-tin altar surrounded by dead men.

One of those ordained with Willie Doyle was John Sullivan who spent nearly all his Jesuit life at Clongowes Wood College in County Kildare. He combined teaching with pastoral ministry and gained the name of being a 'holy man' and a healer. His cause for beatification is under way. Much of his ministry was centred on the neo-classical early nineteenth century public church at the college. To many local people and to many others including myself it is special as 'his' church. (To those interested in Irish history it recalls Daniel O'Connell who prayed there).

Three churches near Clongowes date from the previous century. Straffan Church near the Liffey has '1786' in large letters at its front door. It is in the simple 'penal-day' style, which anticipated modern trends, giving everyone a view of the altar.

The original Staplestown Church on the present site (c. 1750) was low, thatched and T-shaped. In the 1798 rising it was torched in reprisal for the insurgents' annihilation of the garrison in nearby Prosperous. Successive reconstructions made it larger, higher and slated with three galleries accessed by external stairs. In keeping with a tradition that Saint Patrick passed this way it is dedicated to his disciple Benignus.

Rathcoffey Church, founded, it is said, by the Dowager Duchess of Tyrconnell in 1710, at the time when a raft of anti-Catholic laws was being enacted, still has its two external stairs to the galleries.

Let me include here Ballapousta Church in the gentle hills of Louth. This late eighteenth-century church in the penal-day style is associated with the Taaffes, the leading family in the area for centuries who helped to soften the local impact of anti-Catholic laws. (A branch of the family became part of Hapsburg history in Central Europe). Olivia Blake who married into the Taaffes was a special patron of this church.

She is interred here in the Taaffe plot. A few yards away a plaque commemorates her as the founder of the Saint Joseph's Young Priests' Society, which has served priestly ministry in the Church so well for more than a century.

Churches like these, in use for so long, are witnesses to a faith that refused to be silenced and that was focused on the Eucharist. They console and challenge us and unite us with an ancestry to be proud of.

The church at Laytown, Meath, has a remarkable piece of décor: behind the altar is a great plain window, behind it a figureless high cross and behind that the open sea: the whole ensemble reminding us that the God whose Spirit moved over the primaeval waters is the God who engraces us through Calvary and the Eucharist.

On the hilly border between Dublin and Wicklow stands the small wooden church of Our Lady of the Wayside at Kilternan. A delightful church this with its 'alpine' look and devotional décor including four representations of its dedication (two pictures, a window and a statue in the grounds) to suit all tastes! (Not far away and, as we might expect from its dedication, on high ground, is Rathmichael with its fragmentary remains of a church and its stump of a round tower. I remember visiting it with my father in my school days. This ancient sanctuary is still a titular prebend church of the archdiocese of Dublin).

I remember my brief visit to the chapel in Mountjoy prison. The chaplain showed me a room to the side of the sanctuary. This, he said, was where, in the days of capital punishment, prisoners condemned to death and separated from the other prisoners, attended Mass, watching through a hatch. A room for remembering and praying but, for most of us, not for lingering.

Quite different was my visit to Arbour Hill prison where I said my only prison Mass ever. Rarely have I seen a more spotlessly kept sanctuary and sacristy, the sacristan being a guest of the nation from Enniscorthy, County Wexford. With my liturgical tongue in my cheek I used the fourth Eucharistic Prayer, which refers to the Lord coming to set the prisoners free. Many of the congregation of prisoners and warders came to communion.

Two other meticulously maintained chapels I have officiated in are those of the Legion of Mary hostels in Dublin: the Morning Star for homeless men and the Regina Coeli for homeless women and children. They express the deep devotion of legionaries to the Blessed Sacrament, which of course is central in their spirituality. The Morning Star chapel has the privilege of daily Eucharistic exposition. The exquisite star-shaped sanctuary lamp (recalling the name of the hostel) was designed to the specifications of the founder of the Legion, the Servant of God Frank Duff. The reredos picture of angels was painted by a hostel brother and the sanctuary ceiling was crafted by a hostel resident. The Regina Coeli chapel has a prie dieu that once belonged to William T. Cosgrave, one of the founders of the Irish State, who was helpful to Frank Duff in the very early days of the Legion.

Next door to Arbour Hill prison is a small Greek Orthodox Church dedicated to Our Lady of the Annunciation. There in an atmosphere of icons, incense, lights and chanting, led by the appropriately named Father Ireneu ('man of peace') I took part in ecumenical vespers in the week of Church unity.

On to a church of yet another tradition: the Anglican Saint Bartholomew's in Ballsbridge. Its famous clock playing its music every quarter and its bells giving a gala performance on Sunday were part of the local life, part of my early background. No church of my experience has impinged more on my hearing. I remember bursting into the tears the first time I heard 'Bart' chiming midnight: to a child it seemed an awful thing to be awake at that hour. I recall the kindly and popular Reverend Mr Simpson who got into trouble over his 'Romanising' tendencies. Perhaps (the merest thought) he was influenced by the Holy Faith sisters (those of Haddington Road school) in the convent next door. Did they ply him with cups of tea? I'm sure they prayed for him.

But it was not until after my return from Zambia that I decided that it was more than time to pray more formal respects to this landmark of my home patch. I found it well appointed and obviously well cared for – as you would expect from a church, which reputedly had the best-dressed altar boys in Dublin. I seem to remember it as a rather shadowed church, no doubt from the trees on the Elgin Road side. I have some memory of the narrow Calvary window, really seen now for the first time. Perhaps in a flight of personification I could call it a church quietly cherishing its memories of more than a century of service and witness.

Which brings me to another church of Saint Bartholomew, which has been in business (including royal and imperial business) for several centuries: the great redstone Gothic cathedral in Frankfurt-au-Main. I was there in 1994 for the

priestly ordination of Petrus Köst, a German Jesuit who had
been a deacon in Dublin some time before. This is the church
where the kings of medieval Germany were elected and
crowned. They had to be crowned afterwards by the Pope to
become emperors of the Holy Roman Empire of the German
Nation. Papal coronation was later dropped and emperors were
both elected and crowned in Frankfurt. The Blessed Sacrament
chapel was formerly the chapel of the Electors where they
decided whom to elect. My friend and two others were
ordained in front of the high altar more or less on the spot
where the sovereigns were crowned. The modern chapel in the
Jesuit-cum-diocesan college where the new priests celebrated
Mass the next day, backed by hymns in no-nonsense Germanic
style, was a contrast to the history-laden *König und Kaiser*-
haunted Bartholomew-Kirche.

★★★

By that time I was the only member of the immediate family left
in this world: my sister Norah had died the previous year. We had
been very close, the closeness going back to when she was the
'little mother' deputed to take care of the new 'arrival'. I used to
joke in my later and her last years that when I visited her I got
three things: a nice tea, a donation for the poor and a 'ticking off'.
I associate her with three churches: Haddington Road where she
made her first communion, Sandymount where she combined
Mass and music and Milltown where she worshipped for much
the greater part of her life; and with one cinema: the Savoy in its
early years where together we escaped into the musical delights
of *The Desert Song*, *The Rogue Song* and *Rio Rita*.

★★★

People in Church

Quite a few 'people in church' have already appeared in this book. Here I would like to mention those who have come my way since I returned to Ireland from Zambia. It is a joy to see people in church really praying. It helps one's own faith in and devotion to the Eucharistic Lord. The joy is enhanced when the people are young people because an element of hope enters in: they are the future: their presence is good news for the Church and, like the conversion of the sinner, reason for special joy in heaven.

I recall how impressed I was by the young people praying around the Cross in the Dublin Pro-Cathedral on Good Friday: the silence, the reverence, the (literally) personal touch: the hands – and in at least one case the head – on the wood. I have noted that young men (and older men too) are attracted to the shrine of Our Lady of the Way in the Dublin Jesuit church. I like to think that there is an element of chivalry in this: the knight and his Lady, jealous for her honour, sure of her love. Perhaps it's the romantic in me (!) but I warm to young couples in church. I have seen them in several Dublin churches. May life be good to them: God certainly will.

Now and again I have met distressed young people in church: the American student in tears in the porch; the Madrilena sobbing quietly in the half-dark; the depressed student crying his heart out in the Blessed Sacrament Chapel in Trinity College. They were all bringing their trouble to the Lord of Gethsemane and Calvary. That young people should do this is a consolation.

I recall the not-so-young couple exchanging a kiss at the sign of peace at the grotto Mass in Lourdes; the diminutive and assiduous Mass-server and the man of mixed race at the Sacred Heart shrine in City Quay Church; the poor man at Aughrim Street Church who responded to my 'take care' with 'you take care too'; adorers in Haddington Road, Mount Merrion and Newbridge churches; people at the tomb of Father John

Sullivan; the gentle elderly man with goodness, as it were, shining out of his face at Berkeley Road church; the Muslim praying towards Mecca in the Mater Hospital Oratory.

Some names come to mind: my friend Tim in Iona Road and Killester Churches and in the ruined Franciscan friary at Clane, County Kildare; Rory who told me that the autobiography of Saint Thérèse of Lisieux had changed his life; Ashley from India and Lilian from Carlow together at prayer after communion: Ben who had tried a religious vocation and was still happy in his faith; Ramon the Filipino nurse at Berkeley Road; the homeless Jason at City Quay who knew that he was important to God; David the taxi-man from Tallaght, father-confessor to his customers and daily adorer before the Blessed Sacrament; Michael who told me that he owed his conversion to Our Lady; Anton and other members of the Saint Joseph's Young Priests' Society at prayer in the resplendent decorated gold-blue-black Gothic chapel of Blackrock College, County Dublin; baby Ryan with his mother in Saint Thérèse's, Mount Merrion. I recall my friend Jim's marriage to Nessa in that church shortly before my departure for Zambia; and outings with my father to a Mount Merrion that was largely open country; and visits to the chapel that was Saint Therese's predecessor – and a link with the Penal Days in that it was formed from part of the mansion built in 1711: a time when anti-Catholic legislation was in spate.

Two especially moving memories involve children: the young father with his baby (probably fast asleep) deep in prayer before the statues of the Sacred Heart and Our Lady in Aughrim Street Church; and the young mother teaching her small son the sign of the Cross outside Gardiner Street Church phrase by phrase with the hands joined at the end. Teacher and pupil in complete harmony, clearly loving each other: rather like a certain Mother and Child a few years after Bethlehem.

Memorials

Near where I live is a military church in McKee barracks. It is dedicated to Our Lady, Queen of the Most Holy Rosary, the patron of the Irish Defence Forces. It is, as you would expect, splendidly maintained. The flags of Ireland and the United Nations flank the altar. There are memorials to deceased soldiers, including the sixteen who died by accidental explosion in 1941; and a plaque inscribed with the peace beatitude and part of the Our Father: a reminder of the remarkable United Nations peacekeeping record of Irish troops for the past half-century.

Another and very moving 'in the line of duty' memorial is in Saint Columba's, Iona Road 'They are happy whose life is blameless. In loving memory of Brendan Houlihan, clerk of this church 1978-1986, who died aged twenty-six years whilst serving the parish 5 November 1986.' He was in fact criminally and fatally attacked.

One November day I visited the historic church of Saints Michael and John (now no longer a church), then the Travellers' Church, to find long name-filled posters around the altar. The Travelling people had had or were to have their annual Mass for their dead with the names of their loved ones not only in their minds but before their eyes. One way of emphasising the communion of saints.

The cathedral of the diocese of Meath in Mullingar has an impressive list of bishops of royal Meath and of the dioceses out of which it was formed: Irish names first, then Norman and English, later a more inter-racial blend.

There is a similar pattern of names in the Pro-Cathedral in Dublin: forty-nine archbishops from 1152 to the present time. Inset into the outer side-wall of the church is the penal day holy water font of the Liffey Street Chapel, the predecessor of the Pro-Cathedral, dated 1760. A few yards away stand the splendid

sculptures by Conal McCabe of the martyrs Blessed Francis
Taylor, Dublin's counterpart to London's Saint Thomas More,
and Blessed Margaret Ball, Dublin's counterpart to York's Saint
Margaret Clitherow.

The Mullingar and Pro-Cathedral memorials reflect
something of the course of Irish history. A memorial in the
Dominican Saint Saviour's in Dublin is connected with a
sensational event in that history. A plaque in the Blessed
Sacrament Chapel records that the nearby Calvary window is
the gift of Earl Spencer 'In memory of my friend Thomas H.
Burke). Spencer (the great granduncle of Diana, Princess of
Wales) was the British viceroy in Ireland. Burke was his under-
secretary (number three in the British administration of
Ireland) and was murdered, along with the chief secretary, in
the Phoenix Park in 1882.

A couple of years ago I revisited another memorial from the
same period: the beautiful full-figured monument to Aline
(Alexandrina), Countess of Portarlington, in the parish church
of Emo, Laois. She was a convert to the Catholic faith. Her
grave is in the adjacent cemetery. Not far away is the great
house that was her home, became a Jesuit novititiate and is now
owned by the State.

The entrance to Saint Patrick's, Skerries, County Dublin has
an intriguing plaque concerning the (alleged) visit of the saint
and the (equally alleged) theft of his goat by some person or
persons unknown. It shows the goat and has a rather cryptic
inscription in Latin but there is no sign of the national apostle:
we gather from the story that he did not enthuse about the
local morality. There is quite a line of churches along the
Wicklow and Dublin coast dedicated to Saint Patrick: Wicklow,
Kilquade, Dalkey (Church of Ireland), Monkstown, Ringsend,
Donabate, Skerries and of course the cathedral in Dublin – all
evidence of the tradition that he came this way.

The Orthodox crosses over the graves of Russian refugees at Collon in County Louth remind us of a pressing problem and challenge of our time. Set in the cemetery of a Church of Ireland church in a predominantly Catholic area, they invite us to pray for greater love and unity among all Christians.

Lastly, the most extraordinary and evocative memorial of all: the Ark of Kilbaha, which I saw in Moneen church in south-west Clare. A bigoted mid-nineteenth-century estate agent, who apparently had been given administrative carte blanche by the absentee landlord, repeatedly refused a site for a church. Tenants dared not offer their houses for fear of eviction. Finally the parish priest, Michael Meehan, decided, he said, 'to get something … like … a sentry –box'. In this, placed at a cross-roads on the Kilbaha shore-line, with the congregation exposed to all weathers, he celebrated Mass for several years until public opinion, voiced even in the British Parliament, forced landlord and agent to concede a site for a church.

Pilgrim Postscript

I give here some account of ancient church-places, *'áiteanna eaglaiseacha'*, that I revisited or discovered during these later years.

After much searching north of Swords, County Dublin I found a couple of ruined walls in a clump of trees: the remains of the priory and school of the Augustinian nuns' Grace Dieu. It was suppressed by Henry VIII despite an appeal by his administrators in Ireland that it should be spared because of the schooling it provided 'in virtue, learning and in the English tongue and behaviour.' In Portrane a few miles away is the old church where some never-say-die Grace Dieu nuns continued to celebrate divine office. It is said that the son of the acquirer of Grace Dieu used its stones to build a great house at Turvey, inland from Portrane. One of his guests was the now canonised

Jesuit martyr Edmund Campion, at that time on his way back
to the Catholic faith. I once came across a copy of a letter he
wrote from Turvey. I wonder did he meet the nuns of Portrane
or was influenced by them.

The Rock of Cashel has been an *'áit eaglaiseach'* for nine
centuries. Cormac's Chapel, named after the scholar-bishop-
king of Cashel, is a gem of Irish Romanesque. The cathedral is
impressive even in ruins. This was the scene of a massacre of
Catholics in 1647 by the troops of Inchiquin, otherwise known
as 'Murrrough of the Burnings', next to Cromwell the biggest
bogeyman in old Irish folklore. He returned to the Church
shortly before his death, prudently providing for Masses to be
offered for him. The cathedral is also the burial-place of the
remarkable Miler Magrath, Anglican Archbishop of Cashel
(1571-1622) who, it seems, continued to hanker for the Mass of
the Church he had left.

I visited Monasterboice with its scriptural high crosses
(catechesis in stone) and its round tower that stands sentinel
over southern Louth from Ardee of Cúchullain and Ferdia to
Boyne of William and James to eastern sea of Norse and Celts
and pre-Celts. I re-visited nearby Mellifont ('Honey-Fountain':
when it came to naming their houses the Cistercians were
poets) in its meadow beside the Mattock. I stood in the former
chapter house where the monks were told of the impending
suppression by Henry VIII and where, presumably, the actual
hand-over was formalised: the death of the first Cistercian
foundation in Ireland, established four centuries before. The
chapter-house was the scene of another surrender sixty-four
yeays later: that of Hugh O'Neill to the representative of the
English crown. The Cistercians are, I am glad to say, back in the
area, down the road at Collon in the new Mellifont.

The Cistercians had their Mattock and Boyne; their
Benedictine contemporaries at Shrewsbury in Shropshire had

their Meole Brook and Severn. They too were axed by Henry VIII. I recall taking part in an informal Anglican evensong in what is left of the medieval church where so many generations of monks had worshipped. They have made a literary comeback in the splendid Cadfael detective stories by Ellis Peters.

I recall here two visits to Our Lady's Island in south County Wexford. Pilgrimage here goes back at least to the twelfth century to Rudolphe de Lamporte, the local Norman lord, who donated the site to the Church, asked prayers for himself, departed on crusade and got himself killed. Here pilgrims pray – remembering, one hopes, the Norman knight and the Island martyrs of penal times – between the sea and a gentle rise of land, while across the water of the inlet birds come and go in their own sanctuary.

In the more spectacular scenery of Kerry I discovered at Ballinskelligs an Atlantic-lapped priory, related to and successor of the incredible Sceilg Mhichíl out to sea. I viewed the Sceilg from a safe distance and honoured the soldier-angel more comfortably by contemplating the fine Michael window in the local church and the nearby replica of the Sceilg and visiting Michaels' Well which, I was told, had been a Sceilg pilgrim meeting place.

A friend brought me to another well: Tobernalt ('the Well of the Ravine') on the shores of Lough Gill in County Sligo across the lake from Innisfree and Dooney immortalised by Yeats: perhaps the most beautifully situated open-air baptistery (did the great Patrick officiate here?), penal-times Mass centre and place of pilgrimage in all Ireland.

With friends I visited Saint Colmcille's Well at Orlagh on the flank of the Dublin mountains overlooking the Liffey plain. Did the great man come on retreat here from his studies in Glasnevin, attracted by the mountains as reminding him of his native Donegal? A pleasant and perhaps a pilgrim thought for Dublin clients of his like myself.

And down to the Liffey itself at Chapelizod to the gate of the Church of Ireland Saint Lawrence's where I thought of Joseph Sheridan Le Fanu's famous thriller *The House by the Church Yard* which put this village into the history of the Gothic novel. The present church dates from the 1830s though the tower is centuries older than that. The macabre funeral-by-night early scene of the book is set in its eighteenth-century predecessor and the adjoining cemetery. In a later chapter the church is haunted by a 'vampire'.

Local tradition – despite scholarly disagreement – says that the chapel of the Princess Isolde of the Arthurian legend and the Wagner opera was here. There is a documentary record of a priest being appointed in 1228 to a local chapel, presumably on this site. This is the only present Dublin church named after the third-century martyr-deacon of Rome who was much honoured in the early and medieval Church. It seems that his cult crossed the river from nearby Palmerstown where there was a hospital (*leprosarium*) dedicated to him and endowed by the Knights of Saint John (Hospitallers) of Kilmainham. One item in the dissolution of Kilmainham by Henry VIII was the Knights' surrender of their interest in Saint Lawrence's chapel in Chapelizod. Manor Road, Manor Park, Saint Lawrence's Road, Scoil Lorcain and the present church recall his ancient patrimony in these parts: in a sense a Lawrence of the Liffey as well as of the Tiber.

Still in Liffeyland, I visited the 'ecumenical' cemetery of the Church of Ireland church of Saint Mary at Clonsilla, County Dublin where both Catholics and Protestants are interred – one of the Catholics being Patrick Fitzsimon, Archbishop of Dublin 1763-69. A priory of Saint Brigid stood here for centuries, a dependency of the Benedictines of Little Malvern in

Worcestershire and later made over to the Cistercians of Saint Mary's abbey in Dublin. Not a trace of the priory remains; but the dedication of the present church echoes the ancient connection with the famous Liffeyside landmark of medieval Dublin.

I stood in the impressively ceilinged chapter-house of Saint Mary's, now part of a building behind Capel Street, and against the noise of construction and hum of traffic thought of another kind of commotion there on 11 June 1534: young Lord Offaly ('Silken Thomas' Fitzgerald) confronting the royal council, flinging down his sword of office, declaring himself the King's enemy and taking the road to death at Tyburn. (Many years previously I had seen his carved unfinished signature in the Tower of London: 'Thomas Fitzg').

There is a strong tradition that the famous oaken statue of Our Lady of Dublin with a lively Child, now splendidly enshrined in the Carmelite church, Whitefriars Street, came from Saint Mary's. There is a replica in the chapter-house.

Lastly, an ancient church that a friend and I discovered beside a golf course on Bray Head, that great promontory south of Dublin. There at an altar facing the eastern sea and the lands beyond the Mass was said for centuries on the edge of the Christian world.

From a Window
I write this in a room that commands a panoramic view of Dublin with quite a number of its church spires and towers visible, especially when (to adapt Wordsworth) the city like a garment wears the beauty of a sunlit evening.

On the extreme left is the cathedral-like Saint Peter's in Phibsboro with its distinctive shrines of the Sacred Heart and Our Lady of the Miraculous Medal, its rich red-blue-green-gold Sacred Heart window and watered wall-garden dedicated to the departed and bereaved and its Vincentian tradition of clear and informed preaching. Then comes the rather more homely Carmelite-staffed Saint Joseph's in Berkeley Road where the Venerable Matt Talbot prayed. Close to it is the classical Church of Ireland Saint George's (now a theatre), still proclaiming in Greek on its façade the glory of God.

And then the cluster of churches in the 'Liberties', a part of Dublin south of the Liffey rich in history and faith. Christchurch (hidden from view but given here because of its importance), now the cathedral of the Anglican archdiocese of Dublin, was founded in 1038 by Dunan, first bishop of Dublin, with Sitric, Norse king of Dublin, giving land, silver and gold. The following century it was developed with Norman help by Saint Laurence O'Toole and his successor John Comyn. One of Laurence's helpers was Raymond (le Gros) Fitzgerald (ancestor of the Redmonds!). A son of the ancestor was prior of the Augustinian community that staffed the cathedral. The remains of their chapter-house enhance the church grounds. Richard FitzGilbert de Clare, supremo of the Norman invasion of Ireland, was buried in Christchurch in 1177; and the Pretender Lambert Simnel was crowned here in 1487 as 'Edward VI' of England.

Saint Patrick's, the national cathedral of the Church of Ireland, is the massive successor of the tiny church of Saint Patrick *'in insula'* ('on the island') at the place where the saint is said to have baptised and preached. The great west tower dates from the fourteenth century. In this church Henry VIII was celebrated under his new title of King of Ireland with solemn Mass in the early days of its Anglican allegiance. Its founding archbishop was John Comyn, its chancellor-martyr John Travers who refused to accept the religious claims of Henry VIII, its most famous dean Jonathan Swift, its munificent restorer Benjamin Lee Guinness: a quartet of contrasts.

I see the graceful cupola of the classical Saint Nicholas of Myra. This church with its superb artwork (including the *Pietà* by Hogan) is on the site of a medieval Franciscan friary. As well as featuring apostles and fathers of the Church, the splendid ceiling points out that the Legion of Mary was founded in the parish and that the parish once included the Isle of Man. A friend of mine, Tom Kelleher, was baptised here. Every anniversary of what he called his 'real birthday' he attended Mass in this church, kneeling near the font and renewing his baptismal vows.

Next comes the great landmark of the Edward Pugin-Ashlin Gothic John's Lane, the Augustinian church of Saints Augustine and John the Baptist: one of the most beautiful of Dublin churches: its façade is quite breathtaking and its shrine of Our Lady of Good Counsel a quiet splendour. It is on the site, more or less, of a hospital and priory founded in the twelfth century by Aelred the Palmer, perhaps as a thankoffering for his Holy Land pilgrimage from which he gets his name. His hospital lasted for centuries, the largest in medieval Dublin. He deserved to be remembered in the remarkable history of Dublin medicine.

Close to John's Lane is Saint Catherine's in Meath Street, the church of a parish that goes back to about 1300, dedicated to the martyr of Alexandria in the early Church: her cult was probably brought to Dublin by Holy Land pilgrims. Further on is the tower of Saint James's: the apostle is the traditional patron of this part of Dublin. (Do I see it or do I not? Guinness's brewery is in the way). The main door of this austere and elegant Gothic church designed by Patrick Byrne is flanked by unusual corbel heads: the birettaed Canon Canavan, the driving force of its construction, and the crowned Daniel O'Connell, its benefactor and placer of its foundation stone.

Further away towards the hills are Churches of Our Lady in Rathmines (a mini-Saint Peter's) Harold's Cross and Dolphin's

Barn. Nearer to me, on Arran Quay on the site of a penal-day chapel is Saint Paul's (another Byrne church, this one in the classical style) where the Marmions, including the future Blessed Columba, went to Mass. West of that is the remarkable Church of the Sacred Heart in Arbour Hill with its narrow tower standing sentinel, as it were, over the poplar-backed graves of the executed 1916 leaders.

Beyond the former Dublin Cattle Market is our neo-Gothic parish Church of the Holy Family, Aughrim Street. It is traditionally associated with the police based in the nearby Phoenix Park – both the Gardaí and their predecessors. A moving feature is the fifteen benches dedicated to the dead of the Garda Síochána of thirty of the thirty-two counties of Ireland, including the six counties of Northern Ireland. Every November Gardaí come to the church to remember their departed comrades.

Holy Family is also 'presidential' in that the president of Ireland (if a Catholic) is a parishioner. And it is on historic and holy ground: about here an ancient road from Tara descended towards the Ford of the Hurdles where Dublin was to begin, or perhaps had already microscopically appeared; and not far away nearly four centuries ago Blesseds Bishop Conor O'Devany and Father Patrick O'Loughran died for the faith.

I have of course become familiar with this church of a populous and varied parish. I am not one for the ten o'clock Mass, much less one of the faithful few, including my friends Emma and Packy, who attend the seven forty-five (Anne attended too before she left the parish). But I often go to evening Mass and pay my respects to two other friends of mine, Anthony and Thérèse, and to the Mother of us all in her flower-rich grotto garden.

Holy Family Church
From Olaf Road to Aughrim Street they came
Annie and Tom, to pray
and here one summer day
they gave their child to Christ: Moira her name

A church that holds its memories: police
who ask on pews for prayers
the men of cattle fairs
church of Nazareth Three, of holy peace